Deep Ocean
Food Chains

By Marybeth L. Mataya
Illustrated by Hazel Adams

Content Consultant
Jacques Finlay, PhD, Assistant Professor
Department of Ecology, Evolution, and Behavior
University of Minnesota

visit us at www.abdopublishing.com

Published by Magic Wagon, a division of the ABDO Publishing Group, 8000 West 78th Street, Edina, Minnesota 55439. Copyright © 2011 by Abdo Consulting Group, Inc. International copyrights reserved in all countries. All rights reserved. No part of this book may be reproduced in any form without written permission from the publisher.

Looking Glass Library™ is a trademark and logo of Magic Wagon.

Printed in the United States of America, North Mankato, Minnesota.
042010
092010

Text by Marybeth L. Mataya
Illustrations by Hazel Adams
Edited by Nadia Higgins
Interior layout and design by Nicole Brecke
Cover design by Nicole Brecke

Library of Congress Cataloging-in-Publication Data
Mataya, Marybeth.
  Deep ocean food chains / by Marybeth L. Mataya ; illustrated by Hazel Adams.
      p. cm. — (Fascinating food chains)
  Includes index.
  ISBN 978-1-60270-793-1
  1. Marine ecology—Juvenile literature. 2. Food chains (Ecology)—Juvenile literature. I. Adams, Hazel, 1983- ill. II. Title.
  QH541.5.S3M289 2011
  577.7'916—dc22
                    2009051193

Table of Contents

A Deep Ocean Food Chain

A food chain tells us who eats what. It shows how living things need each other. Let's dive down and see what's for dinner in the deep ocean!

In one deep ocean food chain, tiny microbes come first. A shrimp eats them up. Then a dragonfish gobbles up the shrimp. Along comes a giant squid that attacks the dragonfish. But even the giant squid isn't safe. A sperm whale comes and eats the squid for dinner.

Microbes to shrimp to dragonfish to giant squid to sperm whale. That's one deep ocean food chain. But snails also graze on microbes. Another food chain starts. When many food chains connect, they make a food web.

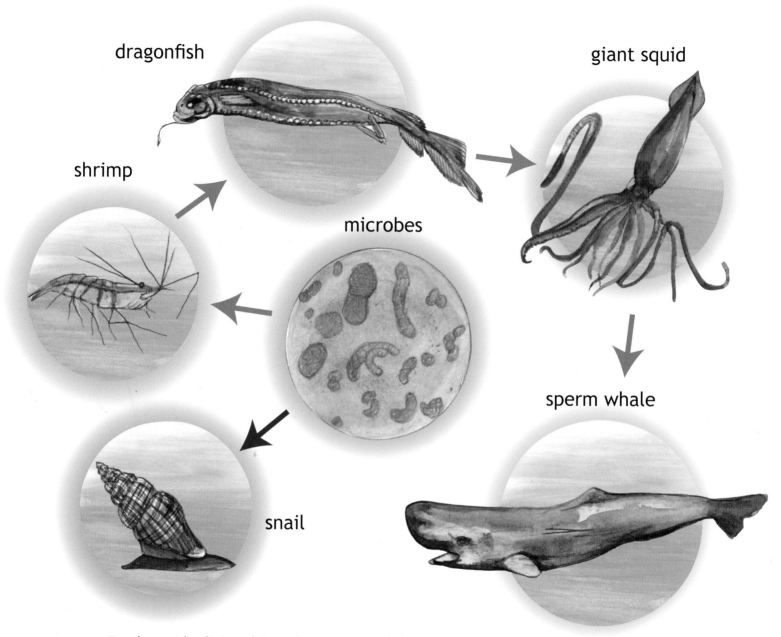

dragonfish

giant squid

shrimp

microbes

sperm whale

snail

Food provides living things the energy and the nutrients they need to stay alive. The arrows show which way food's nutrients and energy move through a deep ocean food chain.

5

The Deep, Dark Ocean

The deep seas are totally black. They lie below about 3,300 feet (1,000 m) of water. With no sun, there are no plants. In most places, the water is almost freezing.

The deep ocean hosts several kinds of habitats. They are like neighborhoods where different creatures live. In some, cool gases seep out of rock cracks. In a cold-water coral reef, fish dart between the bush-like arms.

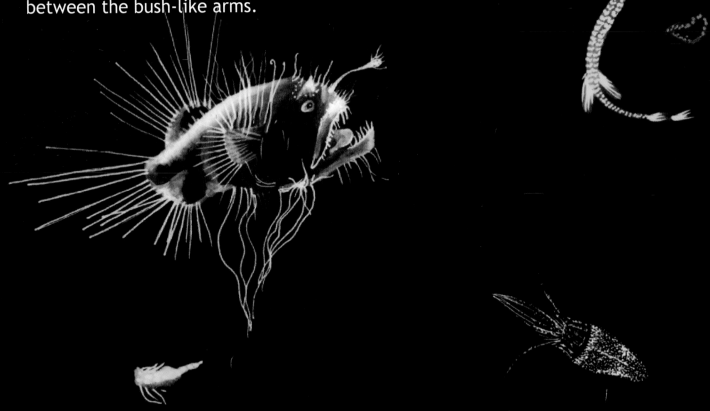

Many deep ocean animals have parts that glow in the dark. They can use their glowing parts as fishing lures. The light can also attract a mate.

Deep ocean creatures depend on life from the top of the ocean. When whales and fish die, pieces of their bones and bodies sink. Dead bits of plants and waste also drift down. These falling bits are called "marine snow." They feed fish, crabs, mussels, and many other deep ocean creatures.

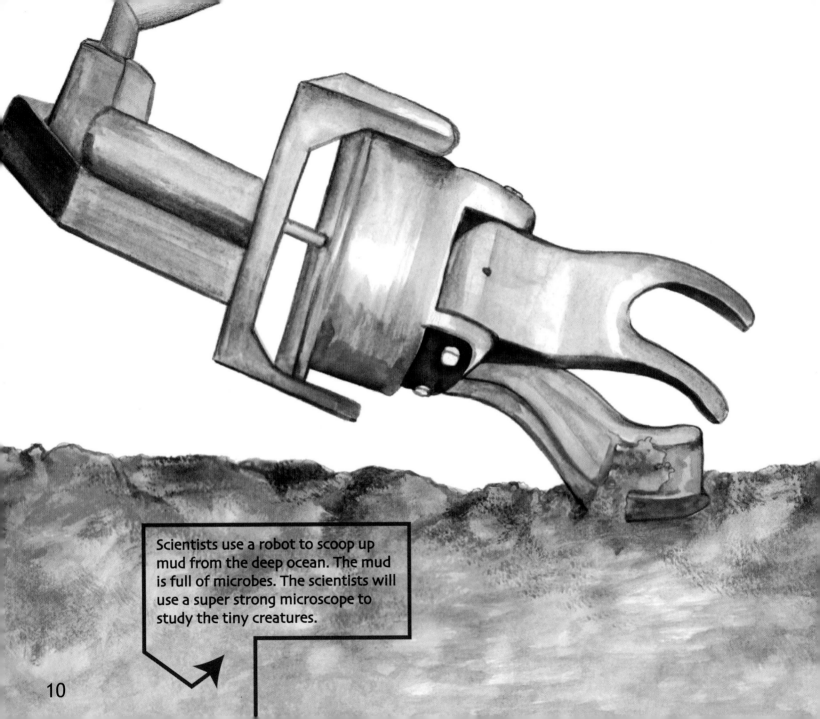

Scientists use a robot to scoop up mud from the deep ocean. The mud is full of microbes. The scientists will use a super strong microscope to study the tiny creatures.

Microbes Come First

Microbes are the tiniest of living things. Some deep ocean microbes feed on marine snow or dead animals. Others make their own food from chemicals in ocean rocks, water, and gases. These microbes are the beginning of a deep ocean food chain.

Grazers Eat Microbes

A shrimp gobbles microbes. So does a snail as it creeps along. These small creatures are grazers. They graze on microbes the way cows graze on grass. They are the next food chain link.

Tiny creatures called parasites may live on a fish. They also feed on the fish's body. Some shrimp feed on parasites attached to fish. The shrimp help the fish by removing the parasites, and they get a meal.

Carnivores Eat Other Animals

A dragonfish lures the shrimp forward with a glowing spot on its head. Then, snap! Its big teeth chomp the shrimp. The dragonfish receives nutrients and energy from the shrimp. Nutrients and energy from the microbes that the shrimp ate also end up inside the dragonfish.

Animals that eat other animals are called carnivores. They are the next link in the food chain.

14

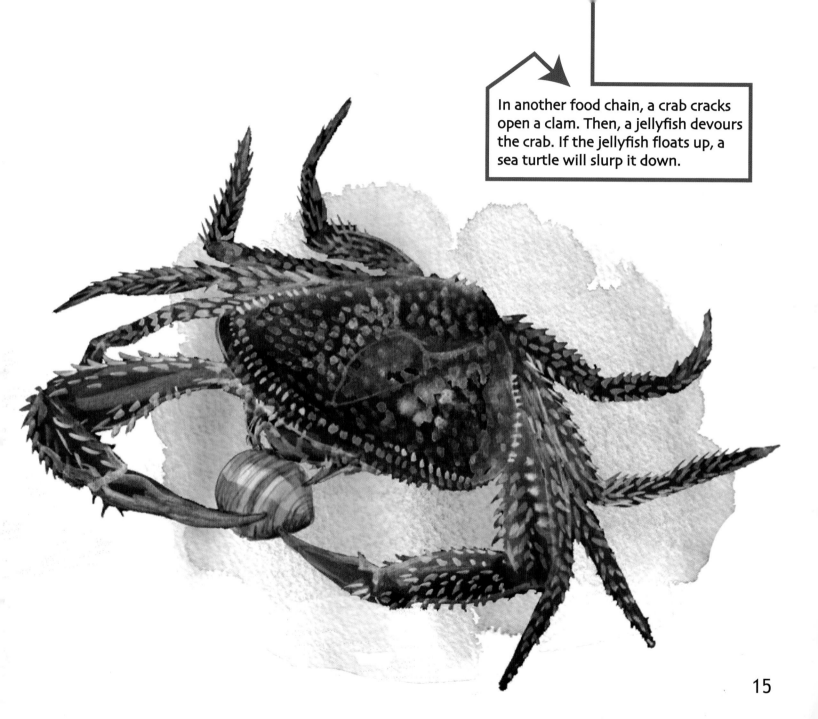

In another food chain, a crab cracks open a clam. Then, a jellyfish devours the crab. If the jellyfish floats up, a sea turtle will slurp it down.

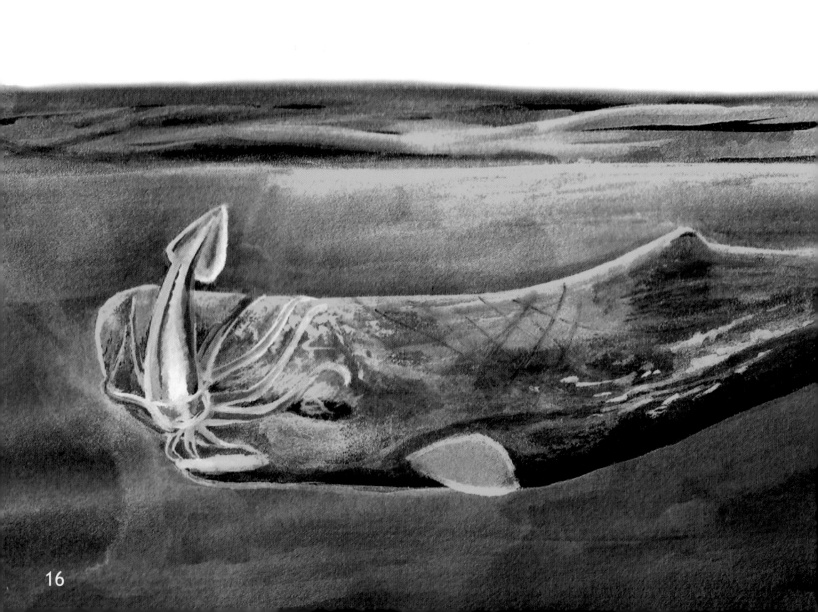

A giant squid zaps the dragonfish with its tentacle. Then a sperm whale dives down. It attacks the giant squid. The squid's tentacles make marks on the whale's skin. But soon the whale eats the squid.

Many carnivores prey on grazers. But bigger carnivores also hunt smaller carnivores.

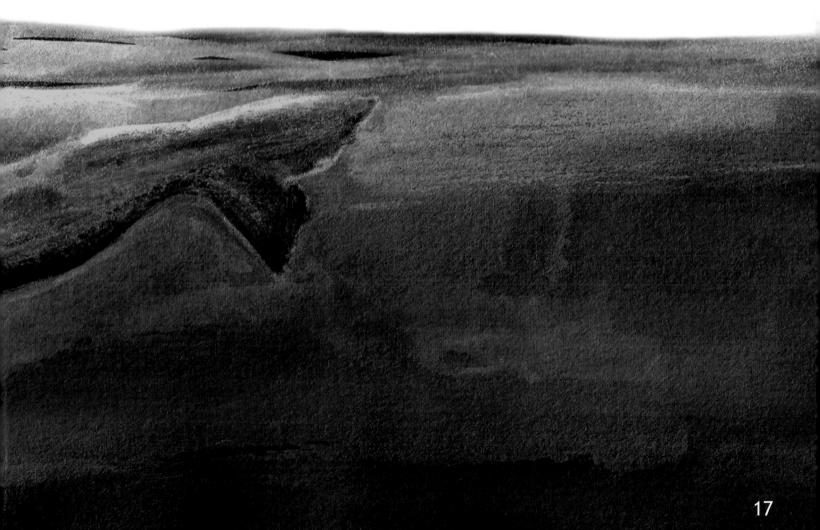

Omnivores Have Lots of Choices

Sea urchins look like spiky balls on the ocean floor. They can eat microbes. They also eat small fish and snails. Food can be hard to find in the deep oceans. Most animals eat more than one kind of food. These animals are called omnivores.

Scavengers clean up the ocean. Think of what would happen if dead fish and whales just piled up. But in the natural world, nothing goes to waste—not even waste.

The Dead Get Eaten

When a sperm whale dies, it falls to the ocean floor. Sharks dive in to tussle over the body. Eel-like hagfish dive in and suck out the whale's insides. Crabs and dragonfish feed on what's left. These animals are all scavengers. They eat dead animals and other leftovers.

Afterward, decomposers move in on the bones and bits of leftover meat. Tube worms, snails, insect-like creatures, and tiny microbes settle in. These decomposers clean the ocean floor of rotting waste. They break down the last bits of food. By doing so, they release nutrients into the water. The nutrients help other sea creatures live and grow.

In turn, decomposers get eaten by grazers, omnivores, and carnivores. The decomposers are just new links in the never-ending food chains.

People and the Food Chain

For thousands of years, people have hunted and fished in the oceans. People are omnivores. They eat plants and animals. They are often at the top of the deep ocean food chains.

Whales are bigger than humans. But people have killed whales for meat and for oil. People eat fish, shrimp, crabs, sharks, and many other sea creatures.

Today, some sea creatures, such as sperm whales, are growing scarce. Laws protect whales from hunters.

25

Some fishermen use fishing nets that drag the ocean bottom. The nets break deep sea coral reefs. They tear up tube worm bushes. These places are home to many ocean creatures. These living things are left with nowhere to live and little to eat.

tube worm
bushes

Be careful not to litter the seashore or throw things into the ocean. This junk sinks to the bottom of the ocean. Sea creatures can eat the trash and get sick. Fish can become tangled in it.

Learn as much as you can about deep oceans and their food chains. Then you can tell others how important and interesting deep oceans are!

Only scientists in their mini-submarines can make it to the bottom of the deep, dark ocean. Scientists find these trips as exciting as going to the moon!

Food Chain Science

Scientists actually know more about the moon than the deepest oceans. But they are eager to explore Earth's most mysterious places. Scientists take little submarines down to the deep ocean floor. They bring lights and take pictures with cameras.

Scientists have found many species around the deep ocean hot vents in the Pacific Ocean near New Zealand. They found giant tube worms that grow together. The tube worms form "bushes" that can be ten feet (3 m) high. These hollow worms have microbes living inside their bodies. The microbes give the tube worms food. In turn, the tube worms protect the microbes.

In the Gulf of Mexico, scientists have discovered what they call "brine pools." These are deep water craters lined with salt minerals. In these brine pools, they have found deep sea mussels, tube worm bushes, red worms, crabs, sea stars, deep sea eels, giant isopods, and some sharks.

With amazing discoveries happening every year, scientists are just beginning to understand how deep sea creatures are connected in food chains.

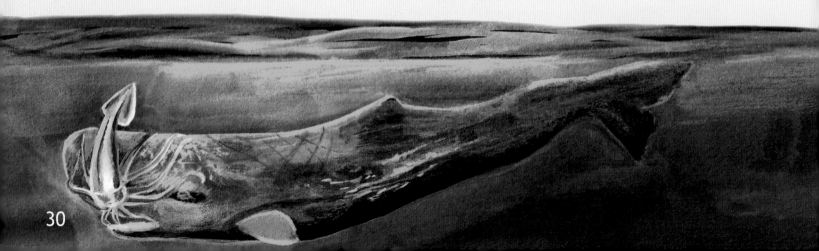

FUN Facts

More than three-fourths of the oceans, especially the deeps, have not been explored. Scientists think that more than three-fourths of the world's sea creatures live there.

More than 60 percent of our planet is covered by water more than one mile (1.6 km) deep.

Several different kinds of barnacles have been discovered near hot deep-sea vents. Some kinds are called "living fossils." They have not changed much since they appeared more than 100 million years ago. That is before the dinosaurs went extinct.

Many deep sea creatures are strange or scary looking. Consider the hagfish that looks like an eel covered in sticky slime. The fangtooth fish has teeth fit for a vampire. The Dana Octopus Squid has light-up tentacles ready to grab its prey.

Ocean scientists think that the deep oceans may have more species than rain forests.

Words to Know

carnivore - an animal that eats another animal.
decomposers - tiny living things that live on the dead remains of plants and animals as well as animal waste.
energy - power needed to work or live.
grazer - an ocean animal that eats microbes.
habitat - the place where a living thing normally lives.
microbes - tiny living things that can live off chemicals or dead animals. Microbes can only be seen with a microscope.
nutrients - chemicals that plants and animals need to live.
omnivore - an animal that eats animals and plants or microbes.
parasite - a tiny creature that lives and feeds on another, larger animal.
scavenger - an animal that eats dead animals and plants.

On the Web

To learn more about deep ocean food chains, visit ABDO Group online at **www.abdopublishing.com**. Web sites about ocean food chains are featured on our Book Links page. These links are routinely monitored and updated to provide the most current information available.

Index